Creatures of
CLASSIC HORROR

A Coloring & Guide Book

Written & Illustrated by Davina Rush

Coloring books by Davina Rush

Creatures of Greek Mythology

Creatures of Classic Horror

Famous Painters in Art History

Alice in Wonderland

Keep up to date on the latest publications at

www.DavinaRush.Com

Dedicated to my beloved daughters—
My own sweet little monsters…

Hailey and Melina

Contents

Coloring techniques

Techniques in coloring with pencil are quite vast, and so we will only touch on this subject briefly. If you are interested in more advanced options, there are a multitude of informational guides and how-to videos available on the internet.

*I do suggest practicing these coloring techniques on a piece of scrap paper before using them in your actual coloring projects.

*For best results, you should use high quality colored pencils.

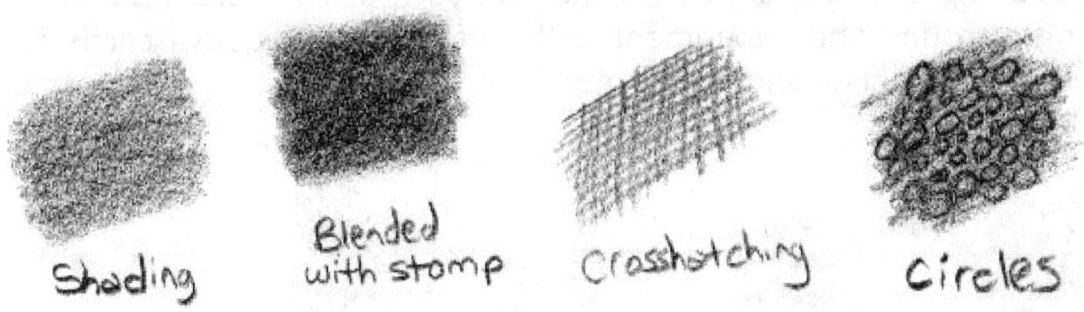

Shading: For filling in large areas of a picture, use the broad, flat side of your pencil led rather than the point. You might choose to follow up with a blending technique as described below.

Blending: For smoothing colors, or to combine more than one color over an area, you can blend the penciled surface with a cotton ball, a blending marker, a stomp/ Tortillion, or a "white" pencil. Some of these methods will only work with the higher quality pencils that you can buy in art stores. Personally, I do prefer the Tortillion blending "stomp" for my projects.

Crosshatching: Use crosshatching for a fabric-like texture in clothing or backgrounds. With a medium heaviness in the weight of your hand, use the point or the side-point of your pencil to lightly sketch vertical and horizontal lines over the desired area. When you have finished crosshatching you can either leave the area as-is, or you can finish it off by blending the entire area to give it a softer more unified feel.

Circling/ scribbling: Using the point or the side-point of your pencil, scribble the designated area with tiny circles, or random scribbles, pressing somewhat firmly so it will show through the over-shading later. When you finish "scribbling" the area you can either leave it as-is or you can go back over the whole area with the blending or shading technique. This will give a nice, bubbly texture that is perfect for monster skin, watery surfaces or for a cool background texture.

You can experiment with many other coloring texture effects such as; veining, cracks, dots/pointillism, little separated circles, squares, spirals, or even rubbing over actual physical surfaces such as concrete, leaves etc. Just play around and experiment with different techniques, search for other methods online and, most importantly, have fun!

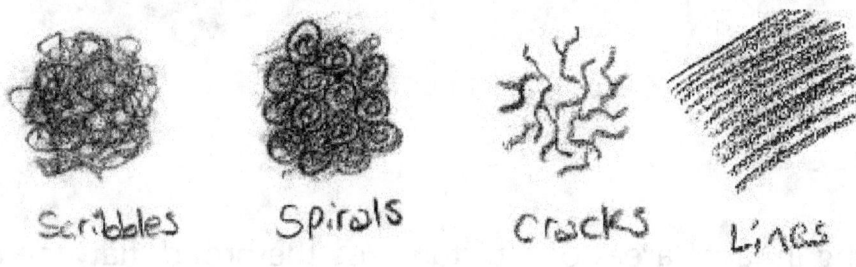

Scribbles   Spirals   Cracks   Lines

Creatures of
CLASSIC HORROR

A Coloring & Guide Book

Written & Illustrated by Davina Rush

Foreword

Born of nightmares and cultural superstition, the many creatures of classic horror have been thriving within the imaginations of men long before moving pictures ever came into being. Fearful stories of red-eyed demons in the night, tales of the dead rising from their graves to feast on the living, superstitious legends of monsters walking among mortals— these are the sinister tales that once terrified people, but now feed the imaginations of theater goers and literary enthusiasts all over the world.

Over many centuries, the tales that so vividly haunted the imagination, slowly evolved from a very real fear into a form of common entertainment; campfire stories, novels and later into the films that we enjoy today. With their main presence now being that of the cinema, many have forgotten the origins of these monsters; thinking them only the invention of Hollywood. In this book, we will take a closer look behind the big screen, at the "founding fathers" of classic horror— from general entities, such as mummies, aliens and werewolves; to the more specific characters, such as Frankenstein's creation, Mr. Hyde and the Headless Horseman. Not only will we be learning about their modern film appearances, but we will also briefly explore the literary history, folklore and superstition surrounding each of these formidable creatures. In addition to all the great information presented in this book, you will also find fun coloring pages and a generous movie list to further acquaint you with each of our sinister friends. Unfortunately, there are so many more films in existence than I can modestly list here, but I do believe I have selected the best of the lot and I hope you will find them quite entertaining as you enjoy coloring the *Creatures of Classic Horror.*

Nosferatu(1922) German adaptation of Bram Stoker's Dracula

Dracula (1931) Black and white cult classic, starring Bela Lugosi

Horror of Dracula (1958) inspired by Bram Stoker's Dracula

The Brides of Dracula (1960) sequel to Horror of Dracula

Salem's Lot (1979) adaptation of the Stephen King novel

The Lost Boys (1987) American horror film starring Kiefer Sutherland

Bram Stoker's Dracula (1992) adaptation of Bram Stoker's novel

Buffy the Vampire Slayer (1992) Dark action/comedy

Interview with the Vampire (1994) based on the Anne Rice novel

Vampire in Brooklyn (1995) Dark comedy starring Eddie Murphy

Dracula: Dead and Loving it (1995) Dark comedy starring Leslie Nielsen

From Dusk Till Dawn (1996) film written by Quentin Tarantino

Blade (1998) vampire superhero loosely based on the comic book

Queen of the Damned (2002) based on the Anne Rice novel

Van Helsing (2004) a monster mash-up, starring Hugh Jackman

BloodRayne (2006) dark fantasy starring Kristanna Loken

Let the Right One In (2008) Swedish film based on the novel

Twilight (2008) based on the Stephenie Meyer novel

True Blood (Beginning 2008) TV series based on Charlaine Harris' novels

The Vampire Diaries (beginning 2009) TV show based on L. J. Smith's books

Dark Shadows (2012) Comedy based on the 1960's soap opera

Vampires

At the mention of vampires, the first image most people think of would be those currently in the entertainment spotlight— Pale, flawless, maybe even "sparkling", supernatural men and women. They draw you in with their unnaturally beautiful faces and charming allure— beautiful angels of death. However, these creatures did not always cast such a sensual picture. The origin of the vampire is long and far away from this shining image of moonlit beauty. Far into the distant past you will find, instead, a much darker and foreboding image of disgust and horror. Rather than a handsome, unblemished seducer, the true vampire of old lore was imagined as a walking corpse with putrid, rotting flesh, who fed on human blood in the night. He was not beautiful or pleasant in the least. There was no charm or elegance— only pure revulsion and terror.

Depictions of these fiendish creatures have been found in the pre-historic art of various cultures. However, the actual lore of the vampire was not recorded until the 18th century, in the wilderness of the Balkans. The Slavic and Romanian people of this region were a very superstitious culture, often turning to their ancestral beliefs, rather than science, to explain the deadly diseases that plagued their communities. Vampirism was a very popular explanation for many ailments during this time.

The terrified villagers were anxious to seek out the demon responsible for their anguish, hoping to save themselves from this dark and unnatural fiend before he could strike again. With this very real belief, it became common practice for suspected graves to be exhumed and inspected. If the coffin was opened to reveal a swollen body, bloated with and oozing gore, it was believed that the deceased had been rising in the night and gorging itself on human blood, infecting others with the unholy curse. Upon these "discoveries", certain rituals were performed in order to "kill" the vampire before he awakened; the most common method being a stake through the heart.

Often, when the stake was driven through the heart, a "groan" would escape the body. To the uneducated ear, this was readily mistaken as the vampire's last breath, when in fact the stake was simply forcing trapped gas past the vocal cavity in a natural release.

This detestable image of a zombie-like fiend plagued the minds of the common folk for ages. The idea of the vampire was not polished up and romanticized until *much* later, during the Victorian era, with publications such as John Polidori's novel, *The Vampyre* (1891). This was the beginning of a glamorous evolution for the undead. With mere pen and paper, these vile gouls were forever transformed into a seductive, charismatic character of great and flawless physical beauty.

While Polidori gave the vampire a fresh new look, Bram Stoker gave him something more that would brand him as the father of vampires, for all time. With his interest in the mad prince, *Vlad the Impaler*, and with the introduction of his book *Dracula* in 1897, Stoker gave the bloody prince of darkness a new and distinguished name to go with his beautiful, reinvented visage. Numerous literary works focusing on vampirism exist as far back as 1748, with Heinrich August Ossenfelder's novel, *Der Vampir*. However, many believe that it is Bram Stoker who has most influenced so many generations of writers and film producers with his darkly romanticized tale and of course the fearsome name itself, *Dracula*.

In addition to the vast selection of books available, there is also quite an extensive list of vampire movies that have been produced. The first known film appearance of Dracula was in *Dracula's Death* (1921), a Hungarian film that has long since been lost to the public. One year later, in 1922, the German silent film *Nosferatu* was released. This film was created as an adaptation for Bram Stoker's Dracula and, even though names and details were changed, all copies of the film were eventually ordered by the court to be destroyed for their infringement on the existing copyright. Fortunately, one copy of the film did survive and has since come to be known as a cult classic; a very influential piece in the massive list of vampire movies and within the horror genre itself.

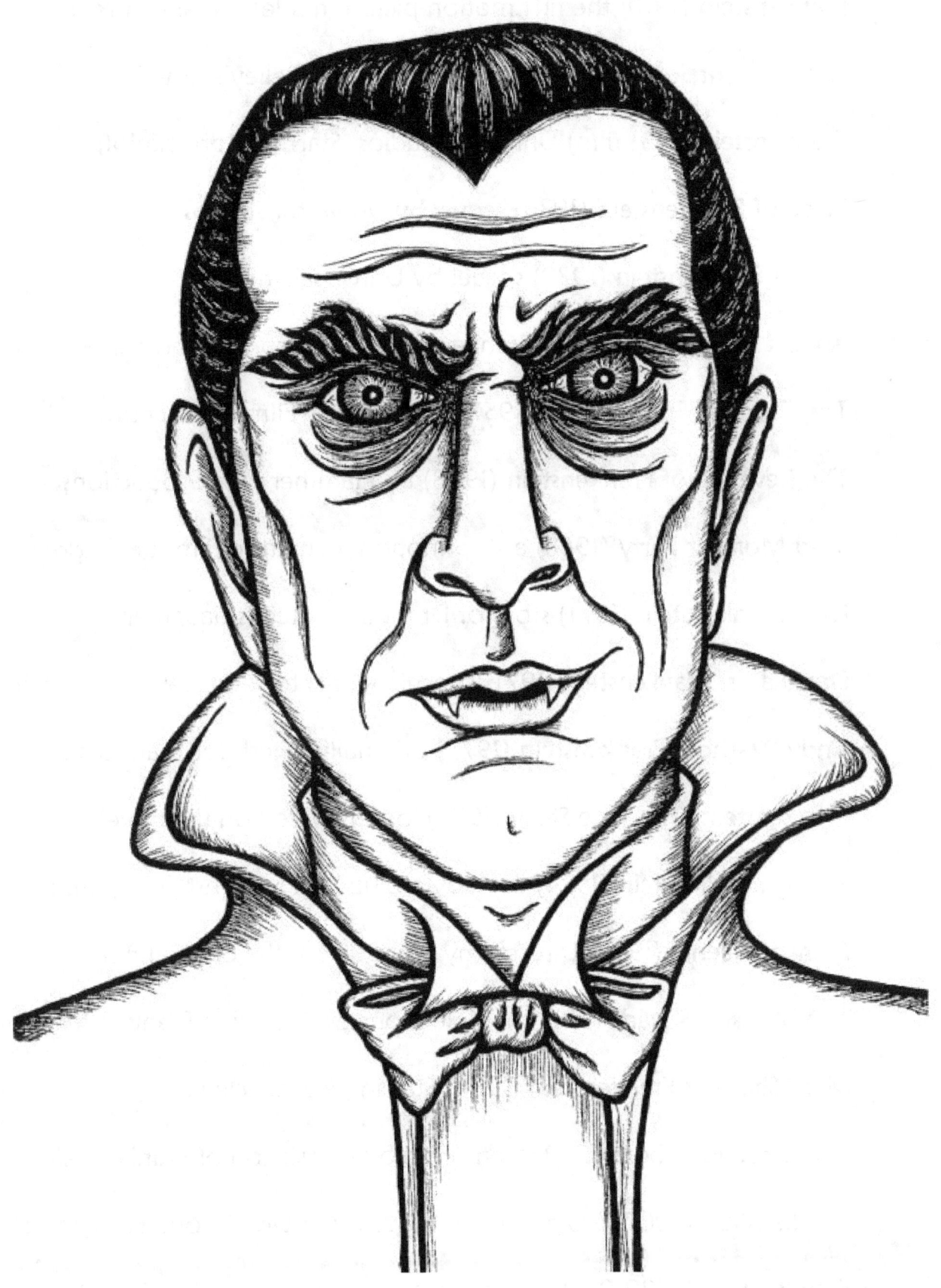

Frankenstein (1910) the first motion picture made of Frankenstein

Life Without Soul (1915) adaptation of Mary Shelley's novel

Frankenstein (1931 film) Universal studios, Starring Boris Karloff

Bride of Frankenstein (1935) sequel by Universal Studios

Son of Frankenstein (1939) sequel by Universal Studios

Abbott and Costello Meet Frankenstein (1948) comedy horror

The Curse of Frankenstein (1957) by Hammer Film Productions

The Revenge of Frankenstein (1958) by Hammer Film Productions

Mad Monster Party (1968) a stop-motion animation film for children

Lady Frankenstein (1971) story of Dr. Frankenstein's daughter

Dracula vs. Frankenstein (1971) Dracula wants to resurrect Frankenstein

Andy Warhol's Frankenstein (1973) originally "Flesh for Frankenstein"

Frankenstein: The True Story (1973) loosely based on the novel

Young Frankenstein (1974) comedy about Dr. Frankenstein's grandson

Frankenweenie (1984) Directed by Tim Burton, the original film

The Monster Squad (1987) multiple monsters including Frankenstein

Mary Shelley's Frankenstein (1994) Starring Robert De Niro

Frankenstein Reborn (2005) a more modern version of Frankenstein

Frankenstein (2007) Made for TV, the story of Dr. Victoria Frankenstein

Frankenweenie (2012) Stop motion animation, directed by Tim Burton

Frankenstein

Unlike vampires, Frankenstein's creation was not born of timeless folktales and age-old superstitions. Rather, he was freshly imagined into being by the young English writer, Mary Wollstonecraft Shelley, as part of a friendly contest. Beginning as a simple wager among her companions, this creature of nightmares would go on to become one of the most notable forefathers in classic horror, both in literature and theater.

It all began in the summer of 1816, when Mary traveled to Switzerland, accompanied by John Polidori and her future husband, Percy Shelley. The three companions joined the famous English poet, Lord Byron, on holiday at his villa near Lake Geneva. Unfortunately, the visit was dampened by foul weather conditions and the friends were forced to remain mostly indoors. To entertain themselves during the dreary days of their confinement, the group took turns reading aloud from a book of ghost stories, followed by in-depth conversations on the subject. One night, however, while gathered around the evening fire, Lord Byron decided on something new to pass the time. He challenged his friends with a contest to see who could write the best horror story— something terrifying to jolt the senses and add some excitement to their days.

Each of the companions spent weeks contemplating ideas and plotting possible story lines, but it was Mary who first rose to the challenge. One evening, after a long conversation spent exploring many grim subjects, Mary had gone to bed with a mind full of dark things. That night she had a vivid and horrifying nightmare of a reanimated corpse and its tormented creator. Upon waking, she quickly began writing down the tale as a short story to read for her friends in their little competition. The group loved it and her husband later convinced her to expand the short story into a full-length novel— and she did.

The finished novel would come to be known simply as, *Frankenstein*. Today, when we hear that name, we instantly think of a big, green, monstrous corpse of a man being brought to life in the laboratory of a mad scientist. However, though commonly mistaken, the infamous name does *not* belong to this undead creation of science. Doctor Victor Frankenstein was, in fact, the name of the scientist who created the monster. In the novel, Shelley refers to the actual creation simply as a nameless "fiend", "monster", "wretched devil" etc.

This dark and chilling tale begins with Victor as a young scientist who is obsessed with recreating natural wonders— particularly, life itself. The obsession grows to maddening proportions as he works to discover a way to resurrect the dead. His experimenting begins with animals, but eventually moves on to a human corpse. Victor pieces together a usable vessel and gives it life, with the expectations that his creation will be beautiful. Instead, he is horrified by the grotesque monster he has created.

The creature is said to stand at eight feet tall, with yellow eyes and thin yellowy skin, black lips and hair, with perfectly white teeth. The doctor is so repulsed by what he has done that he runs from the laboratory, abandoning the hideous fiend. Victor hides away in the mountains, living life in shame and in fear of his creation. The detested monster eventually finds him and, to the doctor's surprise, he expresses loneliness. The piteous creature pleads with the Doctor to create a bride for him, a companion to make his existence more bearable. The doctor agrees, but before he is finished creating this bride he has a change of heart and destroys her. The creature sees what Victor has done and, in vengeance, he kills the doctor's own bride, taunting him with her death. Victor is furious, vowing to rid the world of this evil once and for all. He hunts the "wretched devil" all the way to the far North where, sadly, he dies before completing his mission. Upon Victor's death, his fiendish creation is found mourning over the doctor's lifeless body. Expressing deep remorse, the creature vows to kill himself for all that he has done wrong.

Frankenstein was first published anonymously in 1818. The novel was again published in 1822 with Shelley officially named as the author. A revised, more conservative, version exists, but the first publication is much preferred for its preservation of the author's original voice and vision.

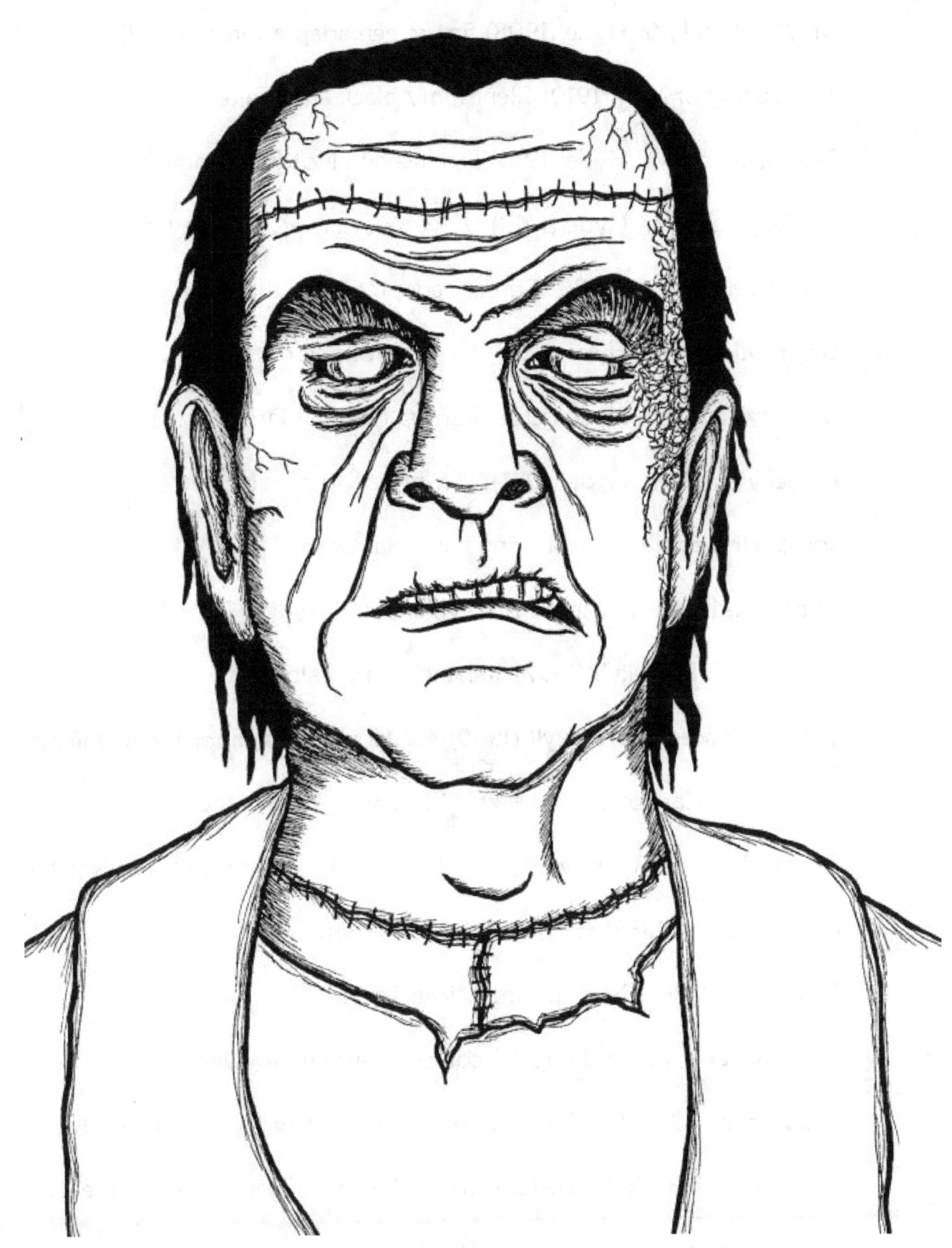

Dr. Jekyll and Mr. Hyde (1908) first screen adaptation / silent film

The Duality of Man (1910) Silent film / black and white

Dr. Jekyll and Mr. Hyde (1910) Produced in Nordisk Denmark

Dr. Jekyll and Mr. Hyde (1913) Universal /starring King Baggot.

The Head of Janus (1920) German adaptation of the novel/ Murnau

Dr. Jekyll and Mr. Hyde (1920) Starring John Barrymore

Dr. Jekyll and Mr. Hyde (1931) Starring Fredric March

Dr. Jekyll and Mr. Hyde (1941) Starring Spencer Tracy

Son of Dr. Jekyll (1951) Starring Louis Hayward.

Abbott and Costello Meet Dr. Jekyll and Mr. Hyde (1953) Karloff

Daughter of Dr. Jekyll (1957) Starring Gloria Talbott

The Two Faces of Dr. Jekyll (1960) Aka House of Fright or Jekyll's Inferno

The Strange Case of Dr. Jekyll and Mr. Hyde (1968) Jack Palance

Dr. Jekyll vs. The Werewolf (1971) Starring Jack Taylor and Paul Naschy

Edge of Sanity (1988) Starring Anthony Perkins

Jekyll and Hyde (1990) Starring Michael Caine.

Dr. Jekyll and Ms. Hyde (1995) comedy starring Tim Daly

Mary Reilly (1996) Starring Julia Roberts as servant to Doctor Jekyll

Dr. Jekyll & Mr. Hyde (2002) Directed by and Starring Mark Redfield

Dr. Jekyll and Mr. Hyde (2002) Starring John Hannah

Doctor Jekyll & Mister Hyde

Mr. Hyde was yet another unique monster pulled straight from the dark depths of a writer's imagination. One of Robert Louis Stevenson's bestselling works, this tale captivated audiences with the terrifying idea that both good and evil could reside as separate entities within a single man; and with the fascinating possibility of purposely splitting those two personalities. Because of this imagined theory and the nature of the beast, this story later came to be commonly associated with the rare psychological disorder known as *dissociative identity disorder*, or more commonly known as *multiple personalities*

In this dark tale of horror, there are in fact two personalities present within the tormented Doctor Jekyll. One of the personalities is good, calm and honorable, while the other is vicious, uninhibited and evil; complete and absolute opposites. Doctor Jekyll desperately wishes to be rid of the evil half of himself— the dark thoughts that plague him. He hopes to remedy his situation by physically separating his "evil side" from his "good side" through the help of scientific experiments. The doctor does eventually succeed in separating the two entities but not quite in the way that he had imagined. Rather than pulling the two halves apart and creating separate physical beings, he instead separates the two conscious minds within his one body. Thus, begins the fight for ownership over the vessel in which they both reside— Doctor Jekyll's body.

In the beginning, the transition is an occasional switch from Doctor Jekyll's mild personality and well-groomed appearance, to that of the loathsome Mr. Hyde with his rough, disheveled appearance. As the story progresses, the doctor is seen less and Mr. Hyde appears more and more often, seemingly taking over the doctor's body and life for himself. Friends and business acquaintances notice the doctor's strange behavior, but they say nothing until Jekyll unexpectedly draws up a living will where he names the stranger, Mr. Hyde, as his sole benefactor. With this shocking and unusual action, Doctor Jekyll's lawyer and long-time friend, Mr. Utterson, becomes suspicious that Mr. Hyde is blackmailing his friend. With this, the lawyer decides to look further into the matter by investigating the mysterious Mr. Hyde. Upon meeting the man, Utterson is immediately disgusted although he cannot name exactly why he feels such revulsion for the strange man. He goes on with his inquiries, later approaching Doctor Jekyll with his concerns, although the doctor assures him that everything is in order and to leave the matter alone.

Dr. Lanyon, a mutual acquaintance of Jekyll and Utterson, dies suddenly after receiving information on Jekyll's condition. Before his death, however, Lanyon sends a letter to Utterson with instructions not to read the document until Doctor Jekyll's death or disappearance. Soon after, Utterson finds the dead body of Mr. Hyde lying on the floor of Jekyll's laboratory, wearing the doctor's clothing. Utterson finds a letter written by the doctor, which he takes home to read along with Lanyon's letter. Lanyon's words reveal that his failing health and death were caused from the extreme shock he had endured at watching Hyde drink a serum and then transform into Jekyll. The letter from Doctor Jekyll explained his experiments, the reasons for them, their success, as well as how things had gone so horribly wrong.

Robert Louis Stevenson, born in Scotland, November of 1850, was a celebrity in his own time for novels such as *Treasure Island, Kidnapped,* and the darkly infamous *Strange Case of Dr Jekyll and Mr Hyde.* While quite sick and bed-ridden, in the later part of 1885, Stevenson had a dream that inspired the unique story of Jekyll and Hyde. After a quickly finished first draft, he had his wife to read over the work and offer her opinions on the story, as was their habit to do. It is said that, after her remarks on the piece, Stevenson later called her back into the room and pointed toward a pile of ash where he had burnt the manuscript, for fear that he would be tempted to go back and re-work the existing words. He immediately started the tale once again, from scratch, taking into account his wife's opinions and suggestions. Later biographers say that Stevenson re-wrote the story in less than six days, while he was in bed, still terribly ill and taking serious medications.

The Strange Case of Dr. Jekyll and Mr. Hyde, was first published in 1886. It was an immediate success and would eventually become a historical fixture in the literary world, painting the face of yet another classic monster in the imagination of man.

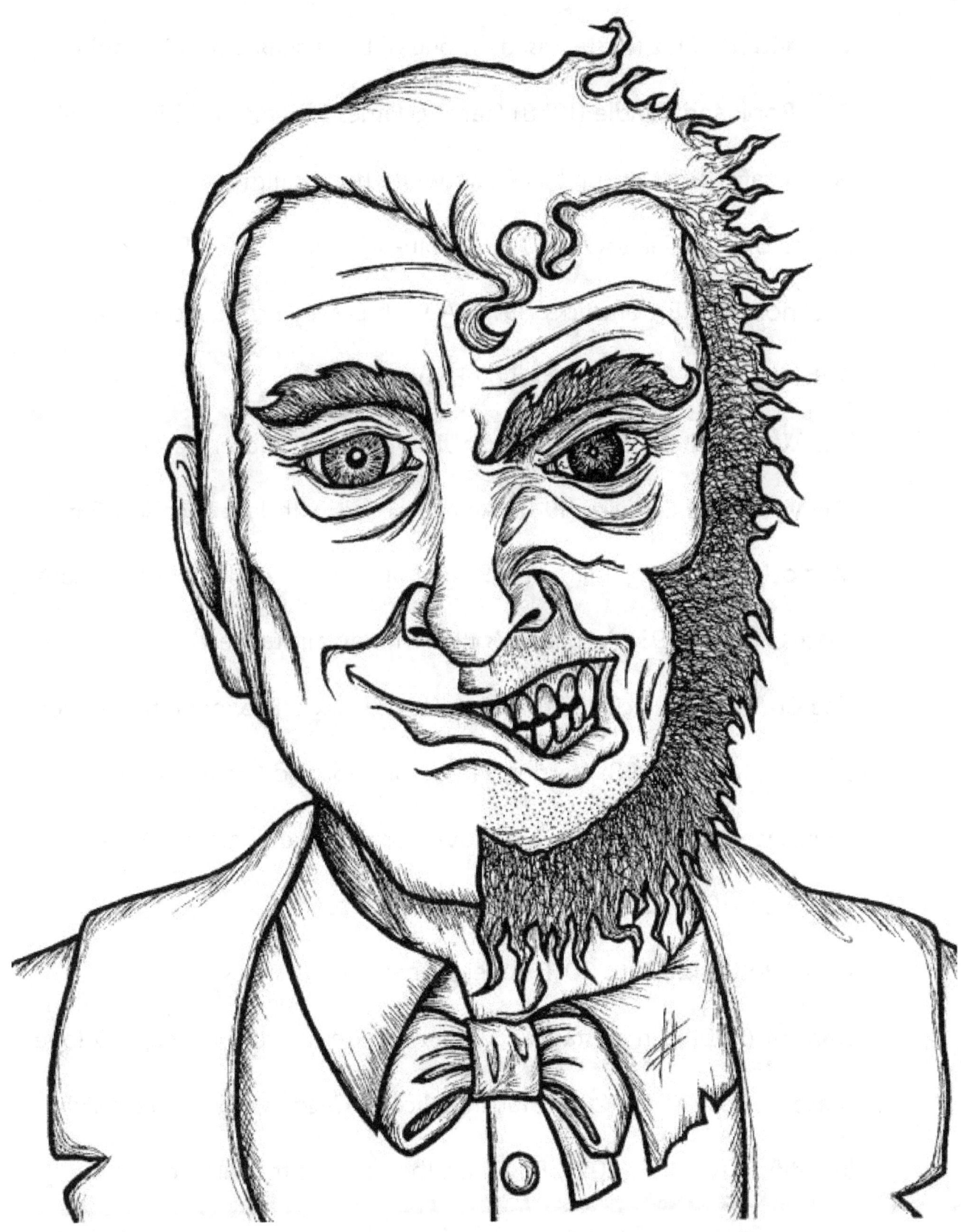

Häxan (1922) retitled "Witchcraft Through the Ages" in 1968

The Wizard of Oz (1939) Based on one of L. Frank Baum's Oz books

Bell, Book and Candle (1958) Starring James Stewart and Kim Novak

Witchcraft (1964) British black and white horror film

House of Dark Shadows (1970) A spin-off of the 1960's TV show

Bedknobs and Broomsticks (1971) A Walt Disney Production

Witching Time (1984) Hosted by Elvira

The Worst Witch (1986) based on Jill Murphy's children's story

The Witches of Eastwick (1987) An all-star cast with Jack Nicolson & more

Warlock (1988) beginning in 1691 Boston, with a warlock facing death

Hocus Pocus (1993) A children's film with an all-star cast

The Craft (1996) recieved first place at the box office, opening weekend

Practical Magic (1998) Starring Sandra Bullock and Nicole Kidman

Halloweentown (1998) A fun movie for the whole family, Disney

Charmed (1998 - 2006) A great witchy TV series

Harry Potter (2001 to 2011) An eight-part movie series

Stardust (2007) An all-star cast with a wonderful story of magic & love

Season of the Witch (2011) Starring Nicolas Cage as a Teutonic Knight

Beautiful Creatures (2013) Based on the book of the same name

Oz the Great and Powerful (2013) Going back to the wizard's arrival

Witches

Witches may very well be one of the most common and oldest known supernatural characters in film, literature and throughout history around the world; second only perhaps to demons and ghosts. From the beginning of recorded history, many cultures have practiced various rituals for religious purposes, medicinal purposes and for divination. These arts were once commonly accepted, and the practitioners were revered as wise men/women, healers or shamans etc. However, even during these ancient times of acceptance, they did invoke a small measure of fear, in addition to the respect they were paid. This minor apprehension soon became a great terror with the spread of new belief systems and cultural changes. Given the label of "witchcraft" by religious communities, ancient tribal practices were quickly deemed unholy, malicious and unnatural. To be named a witch during this time was a punishable crime, where offenders might be burned, hanged or drowned.

There were two main views held by old society concerning the naming of a witch. Many people feared the supposed powers of the witch, claiming that they were in league with the Devil and were to blame for most illnesses and misfortune that fell upon the community. According to this view, it was believed that accused witches should not be 'suffered to live'. On the other hand, there were many who viewed witchcraft as impossible and complete nonsense. Those who refused to believe in these superstitions, created many decrees in various areas that outlawed the prosecution, torture or execution of persons accused of witchcraft.

Singular executions of accused witches were common during these times, such as with King James's execution of two women whom he believed had performed sorcery on him. He accused the women of creating a storm, with the hopes of sinking his ship in order to drown he and his wife, Queen Anne. Then there are other cases in history where the accusations were on a grander scale and out of control. In these cases of mass hysteria, thousands of innocent lives were claimed over foolish accusations and pure spite. During these witch hunts, spanning from the late 1400's into the 1700's, throughout Europe and into North America, it is recorded that well over 40,000 people (both men and women) were imprisoned, tortured and executed after being accused of using witchcraft.

Since those dark times in history, the idea of witchcraft has greatly evolved. There are many cultures today who practice earth-based religions that would have once been persecuted for their beliefs, but now enjoy the freedom to do as they please, so long as they harm no one. However, even in these modern times of acceptance, there are many societies that remain adamantly against these practices. In these cultures, surprisingly, witch-hunts still exist, where people are accused and punished for the "crime" of sorcery and witchcraft. Africa, New Guinea, India and Saudi Arabia are just a few of the places where witchcraft is still greatly feared and blamed for many illnesses and misfortunes, just as they were so long ago. Much like the old witch-hunts of Salem, the accusers are often speaking out of fear or pure malice, knowing that the accused will be driven from their homes to exile, suicide or a violent execution.

Much like with anything else in life, there will always be different views on witchcraft; some people will be more accepting or dismissive, while others will continue to fear and hate what they do not understand. This is how the witch has been portrayed in the literary and film genres as well— through multiple points of view. Sometimes she is illustrated as an ugly, fearful and unholy bride of the Devil, as with the witches of the coven in *Rosemary's baby* or the wicked witch in *The wizard of OZ*. And sometimes, she is portrayed as a beautiful priestess of nature or a heroine of sorts, such as Morgana and her fellow priestesses in *Mists of Avalon* or the three sisters in the popular TV show *Charmed*. Then, at other times, she is simply portrayed as a common, modern woman tucked away unnoticed in an ordinary domestic environment such as Tabatha in *Bewitched* or the Spellman family in the TV show *Sabrina*.

Throughout society and in entertainment history, the witch (as with many of the monsters in this book) has found herself on both ends of the spectrum; both loved and hated. But, above all opinion, good or bad, she has always found herself very much right in the spotlight, on a cinema pedestal along with her other supernatural friends.

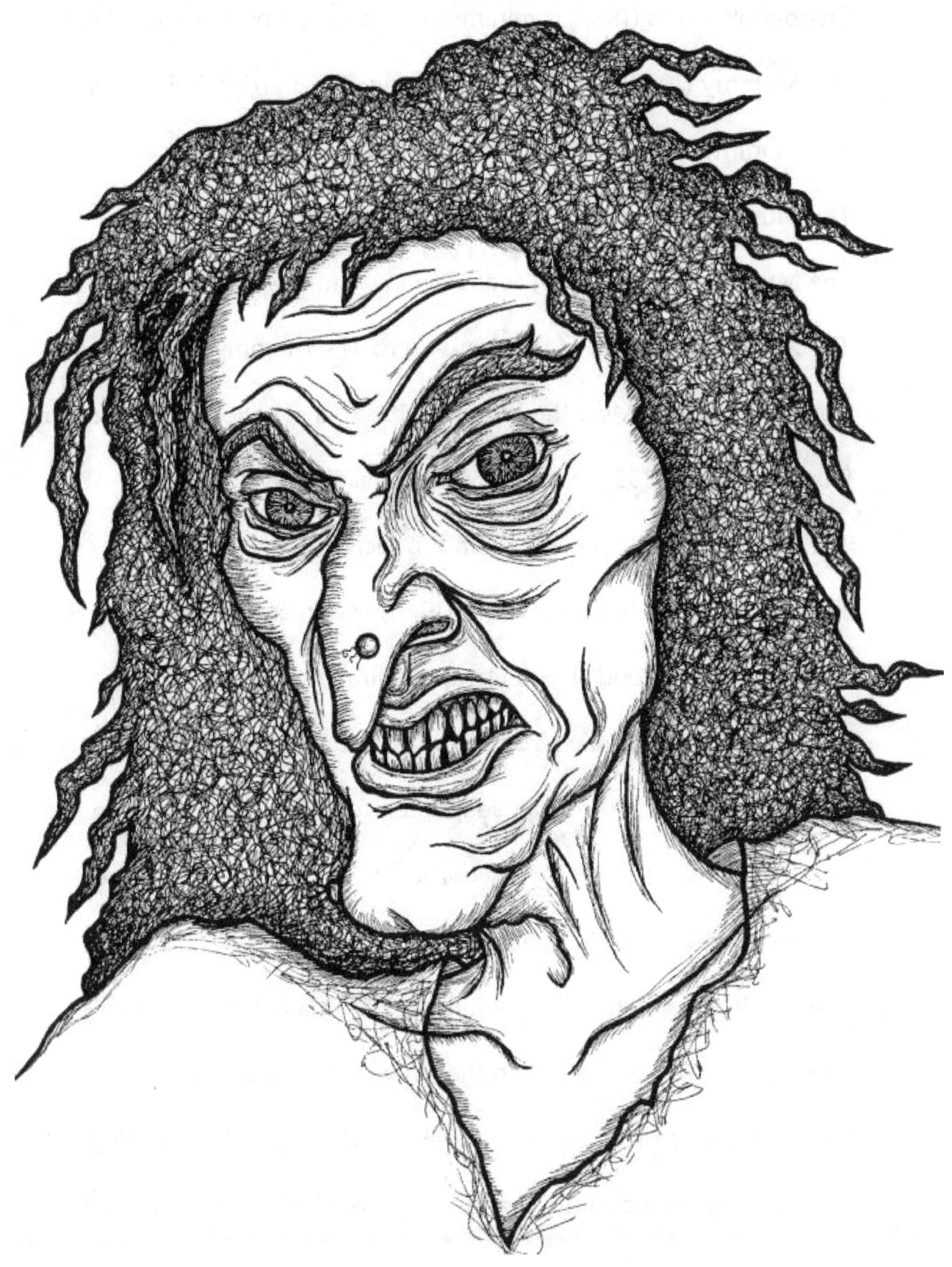

Cleopatra's Tomb (1899) 2 minute short, directed by Georges Méliès

The Mummy (1932) Universal Film Production Starring Boris Karloff

The Mummy's Hand (1940) Universal Studios

The Mummy's Tomb (1942) Sequel to The Mummy's Hand

The Mummy's Ghost (1944) Sequel to the Mummy's tomb

The Mummy's Curse (1944) Follow-up to The Mummy's Ghost

Abbott & Costello Meet the Mummy (1955) final Abbott & Costello film

Pharaoh's Curse (1957) Starring Mark Dana and Ziva Rodann

The Mummy (1959) Hammer Film Productions

The Curse of the Mummy's Tomb (1964) Hammer Film Productions

The Mummy's Shroud (1967) Hammer Film Productions

Blood from the Mummy's Tomb (1971) Based on Bram Stoker's novel

The Awakening (1980) Novel adaptation for "The Jewel of Seven Stars"

The Monster Squad (1987) comedy/horror film by Tri-Star Pictures

The Mummy Lives (1993) Cannon Pictures

Bram Stoker's Legend of the Mummy (1997) made for cable movie

The Mummy (1999) first film in the Universal Pictures trilogy

The Mummy Returns (2001) second in the Universal Pictures trilogy

The Mummy: Tomb of the Dragon Emperor (2008) third in the trilogy

Mummies

Zombies, vampires and Dr. Frankenstein's fiend were all creatures that had once been human, having fallen in death and then resurrected through infection or science. To be resurrected after death as an animated corpse seems to be a common, reoccurring theme in most classic horror and dark folk lore— the mummy is yet another of the walking dead.

Mummies were not actually created to be monsters, believe it or not. These bandage-wrapped bodies, creepy as they are, were originally part of an ancient burial method, most commonly associated with the Egyptians (although mummification was practiced in other cultures as well). Upon death, according to Egyptian ritual, the human body was taken to a special temple for preparation. The internal organs of the body, such as the liver, intestines and brains, were surgically removed, dehydrated, wrapped and then placed back inside the corpse or inside canopic jars to be buried with the body. The corpse itself was dried out with natron so that it would not decompose from moisture, and then it was bathed in oils the keep the skin elastic. After all these steps were taken, the prepared body was then wrapped in linens and laid to rest in its decorated sarcophagi, within the personal or family burial chamber.

The mummified monster that we are familiar with today is not the same as the one in this quiet burial ceremony. Instead, we are more familiar with a grotesque, resurrected, bandaged corpse walking about, arms raised out in front of his body while he moans in discontent. However, it was not until the early 1800's that this vision of the mummy was introduced to the public imagination. One of the earliest examples of mummy-themed horror is in the novel, The Mummy! : Or a Tale of the Twenty-Second Century, written by Jane C. Loudon in 1827.

During the 20th century, the notion of mummies rising from their sarcophagi to walk among the living were further popularized through literature and film, more specifically with the *Universal Studio* monsters.

In 1932, Boris Karloff starred in one of the first major, full-length films that focused on the idea of mummies in horror. The film was inspired by the well-publicized opening of Tutankhamen's tomb in 1922, and the popular belief in the "curse of the pharaohs". In *The Mummy*, Karloff plays the ancient Egyptian priest, Imhotep, who had long since been mummified alive as a punishment for stealing the pharaoh's wife. When one of the archeologists recklessly reads aloud from a scroll found in the tomb, Imhotep awakens as a terrifying mummy, resurrected by the spell. After escaping, the resurrected priest goes in search of his reincarnated lover, while the men hunt for him and battle to return him to the grave.

While this groundbreaking movie was solely a fictional creation, there is some truth to the belief of "cursed" tombs. There is no proof that these curses have any real affect, but there have been rare occasions where burial chambers do in fact contain hieroglyphic inscriptions that warn of a curse on any who would disturb the sacred resting place of the dead. Although, even without the written inscriptions, there seemed to be a general superstition that anyone disturbing a tomb would be punished in some way for desecrating the grave and disturbing the dead; especially the tomb of a pharaoh.

The most publicized case of a supposed curse occurred in 1922, when a few members of Howard Carter's archeology team died "mysteriously" after opening the tomb of Pharaoh Tutankhamen. Lord Carnarvon was the first in the team believed to fall victim to the "curse", having been bitten by a mosquito, resulting in an infection, severe blood poisoning and ultimately his death. Howard Carter, on the other hand, the person who should have been most quickly affected by this curse, since he had led the expedition, seemed to enjoy a completely normal and full life. In fact, Carter lived another 17 years after and died of natural causes at the age of 64. Ultimately, the curse of Tutankhamen is said to be no more than a public exaggeration, since there had been 22 people present when the tomb was opened and, by 1934, only six of those people had died, and all from natural causes.

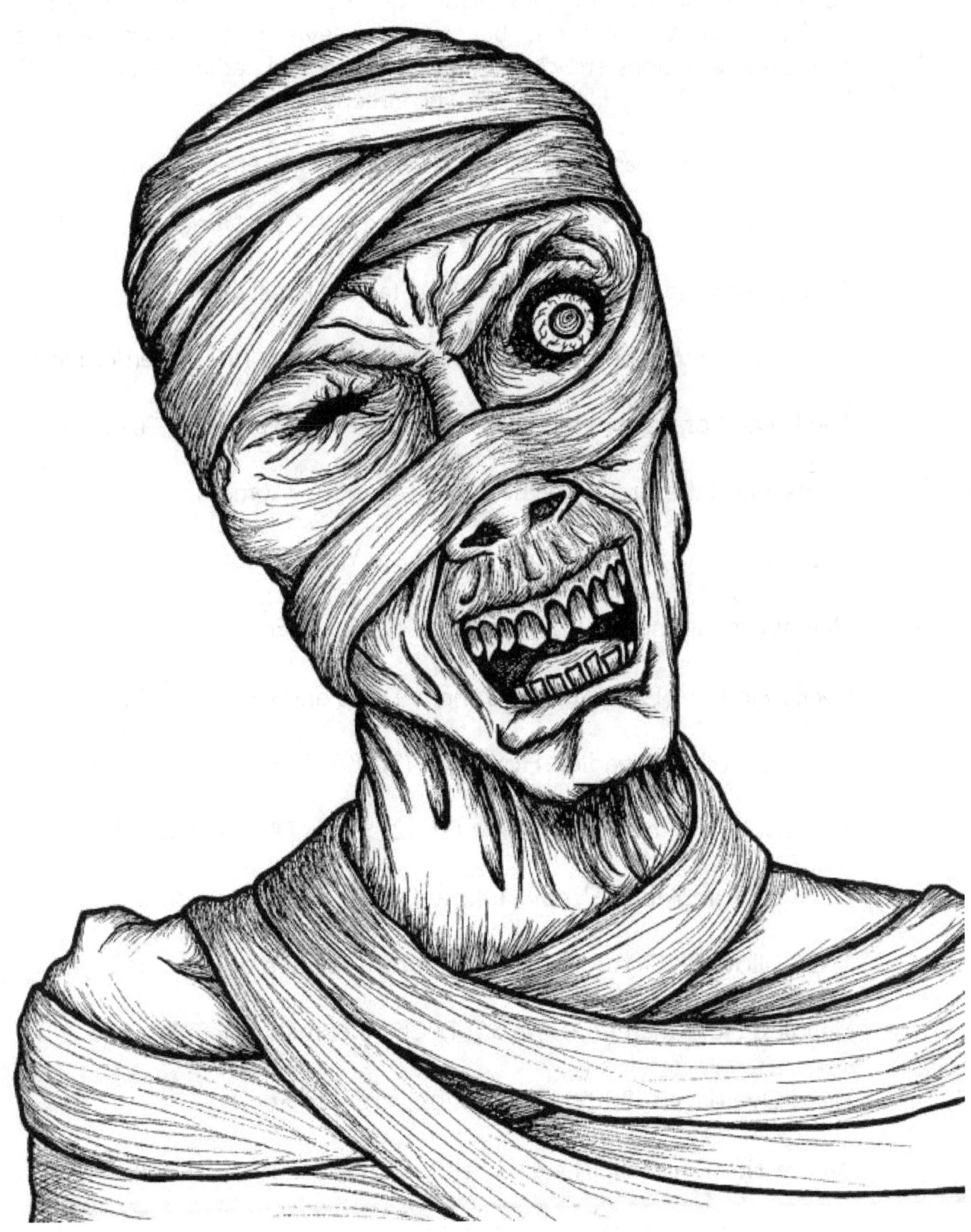

The selection for movies featuring headless horsemen was quite limited. For that reason, this list does include quite a few examples that are not full-length movie features, but rather television series appearances, cartoon adaptations etc. of the two best known headless horsemen; the Hessian from Sleepy Hollow and The Green Knight.

The Headless Horseman (1922) Starring Will Rogers, one of the first adaptations

The Adventures of Ichabod and Mr. Toad (1949) A Disney Production

Gawain and the Green Knight (1973) Starring Nigel Green

Sword of the Valiant (1984) Starring Sean Connery (the Green Knight)

The Legend of Sleepy Hollow (1985) Tall Tales & Legends: S1/Ep1

Gawain and the Green Knight (1991) Made for TV movie

The Tale of the Midnight Ride (1994) Are You Afraid of the Dark? S3/Ep1

Halloween Hound (1998) Wishbone S2/Ep1 & Ep2

Sleepy Hollow (1999) Starring Johnny Depp and Christina Ricci

The Night of the Headless Horseman (2000) Computer animation

Sir Gawain and the Green Knight (2002) James D'Arcy, Anton Lesser The

Haunted Pumpkin of Sleepy Hollow (2003) Animation for kids

The Hollow (2004) Story of Ian Cranston, relative of Ichabod Crane

Headless Horseman (2007) A SCI-FI Channel made for TV movie

Head Over Heels (2009) Ghost Whisperer S5/Ep6

Where There's a Will, There's a Fae (2010) Lost Girl S1/Ep2 brief appearance

Sleepy Hollow (2013) A new FOX TV series premiering September 2013

Headless Horsemen

You may remember the headless horseman from *The Legend of Sleepy Hollow*, but did you know that there are many other tales of headless hauntings all over the world and throughout history?

In Ireland, for example, there roams a dark spirit of fairy lore called the Dullahan. Legend says that this ominous figure rides a horse as black as night, carrying his detached head beneath one arm while wielding a whip of human bone in the other hand. The Dullahan rides fiercely through the woods, stopping only on occasion to call out a name; whatever unlucky name he shouts into the night is doomed to die immediately. In Scotland, there are tales of yet another headless horseman; a simple legend of a man killed in battle, decapitated, and cursed to haunt the Isle of Mull for all of time in search of his lost head. And then, in German folk lore, as kept by the Brothers Grimm, there are two other accounts of headless horsemen. One of these hauntings is a benign apparition of a headless man atop a gray horse, roaming the river shores as an omen of ill tidings; the other haunting was known as the "wild huntsman" and was much like the Irish Dullahan.

The best-known story of a headless horseman in folklore is that of *The Legend of Sleepy Hollow*, a tale written by the American author Washington Irving. The beheaded ghost in this tale is a nameless Hessian soldier who was one of many men killed in battle— decapitated by a stray cannonball of all things! This particular horseman is not a benign specter, however, as the ones we spoke of previously. This creature of horror is much more violent, as he plagues a quiet settlement in Tarrytown, New York. In this story, after being told the spooky tale of the horseman, Ichabod Crane ignores the warnings and makes his way home through the haunted glen. To his utter horror, he is met by a dark and eerily quiet man atop a horse, cloaked and— upon closer investigation— *missing his head!* Ichabod rides for his life, fast and hard for the bridge that the Hessian is said to be unable cross. To Ichabod's unhappy shock, the Hessian does cross the bridge and the story ends with the young lad's mysterious disappearance.

Aside from the legend of Sleepy Hollow, you may also remember another headless horseman from the well-known story of *Sir Gawain and the Green Knight*. In this story, the headless horseman is not a ghostly apparition, but instead appears as a seemingly flesh and blood knight. This mysterious horseman arrives uninvited in the court of King Arthur, where he presents a strange and dangerous challenge to the king. His game is quite strange, as he invites any knight of the court to step forward and strike at his neck with an ax, but only if the dealer of the blow will, in turn, agree to allow the Green Knight the same favor in one years' time. Sir Gawain accepts the challenge on his king's behalf, as no other knight will step forward. Gawain beheads the Green Knight with one swing of the ax and for a moment believes the man to have been a complete fool, as he lay decapitated for all to see. However, to everyone's shock, his body stands up unaffected and walks over to retrieve his severed head. As the knight is leaving the court full of astonished witnesses, he reminds Gawain of his terms, promising to collect his due in one years' time,

For honors' sake, Gawain must uphold his end of the bargain, and so in one years' time he leaves Camelot in search of the Green Knight. He has accepted his fate and plans to put his neck at the mercy of the man's ax, as they had agreed in their ghoulish game. As he kneels before the strange knight, he is dealt only a small wounding scratch on the back of his neck and allowed to live with a hearty laugh from the Green knight. The entire game turns out to be only a terrible trick played by the sorceress Morgan le Fay, King Arthur's half-sister.

In popular fiction, there have been many more stories of headless spirits, most of them completely harmless such as "nearly headless Nick" in the *Harry Potter* series. The headless horseman of Sleepy Hollow, however, is one truly sinister soul, relentless in his eternal vengeance.

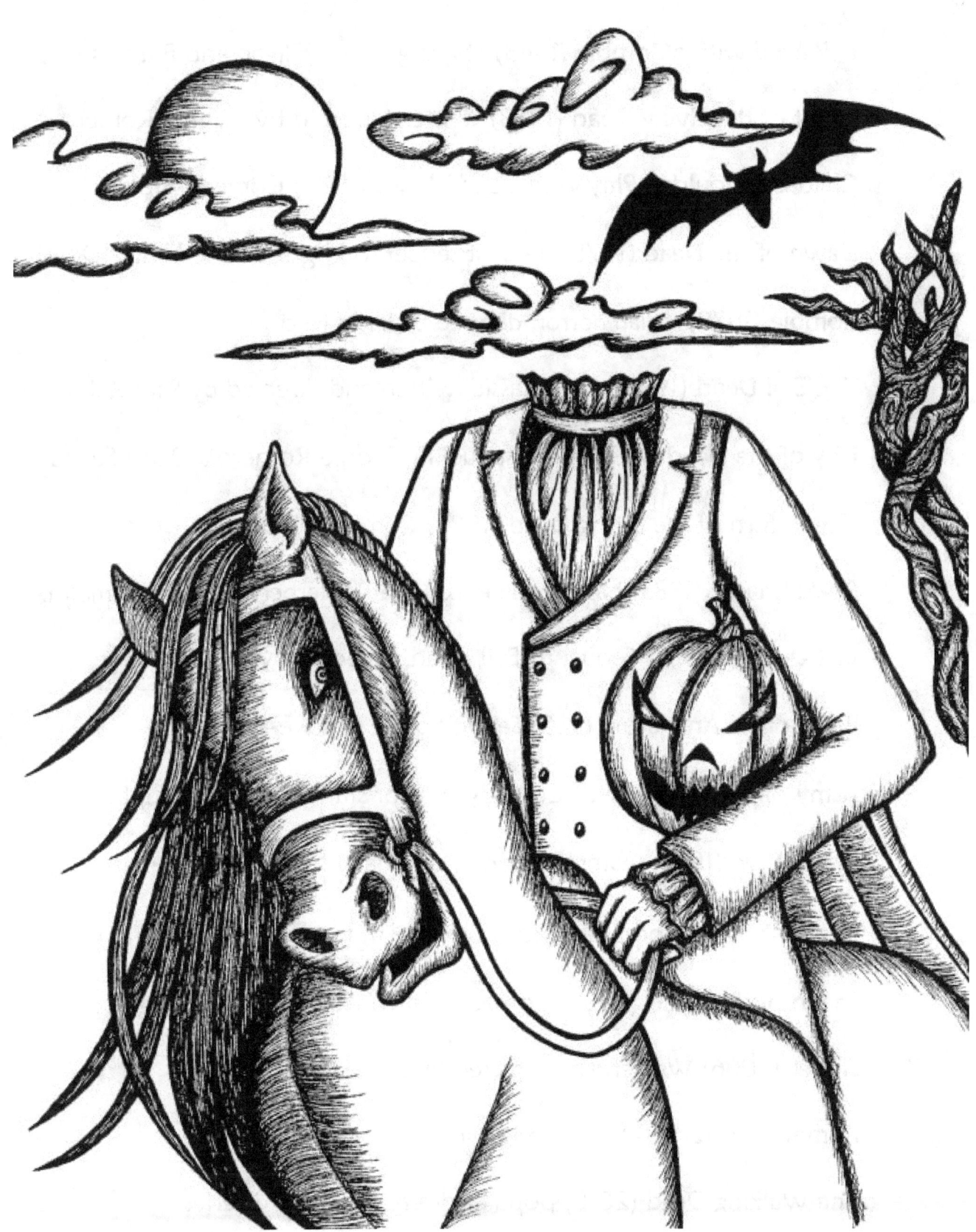

White Zombie (1932) Starring Bela Lugosi, following the Bokor version

I Walked with a Zombie (1943) Starring James Ellison and Frances Dee

Night of the Living Dead (1968) written/directed by George Romero

Children Shouldn't Play with Dead Things (1973) Comedy/Horror

Dawn of the Dead (1978) the first sequel to Night of the Living Dead

Zombie (1979) Italian horror, directed by Lucio Fulci

The Evil Dead (1981) a cult-classic written and directed by Sam Raimi

Day of the Dead (1985) third sequel in George Romero's Dead Series

The Return of the Living Dead (1985) Comedy/ Horror

Re-Animator (1985) based on H.P. Lovecraft's Herbert West—Reanimator

Evil Dead II (1987) Sequel to Evil Dead, Directed by Sam Raimi

Bride of Re-Animator (1989) Sequel to the first Re-Animator

Army of Darkness (1992) Comedy/Horror starring Bruce Campbell

Dead Alive (1992) Comedy/Horror originally titled Braindead

Resident Evil: Apocalypse (2004) the 2nd in the Resident Evil film series

Shaun of the Dead (2004) Comedy/Horror starring Simon Pegg

Slither (2006) Written and directed by James Gunn

Zombieland (2009) With Woody Harrelson and Emma Stone

The Walking Dead (2010) popular drama/horror TV Series

Zombies

When we think of zombies, the most common image that pops in our head is that of a mindless, reanimated corpse, hungry for human flesh. You know the story— bitten or scratched by a zombie, the infection killing its victim, only to reanimate the body as one of the walking dead. Most all science fiction movies depict zombies in just this way. However, the original act of zombification did not involve a virus at all. The true story of the zombie is *much* scarier, as it is based on real-life accounts.

Rather than an apocalyptic America, the true horror of the zombie began in places like Haiti and Africa. You may be disappointed though, since these original zombies are neither grotesque or hungry for brains. In fact, they aren't scary at all. In these cultures, the idea of the zombie itself is not a fearful thing. However, the thought of being *turned into a zombie* and enslaved as one is a very real fear among these people, even today.

It is very taboo and highly frowned upon, but there are still "Bokors", or voodoo sorcerers, who continue this dark practice. There's no magic to it, contrary to what they might have you believe; just simple trickery, kidnapping and enslavement. The Bokor begins by making a mixture of secret powders that he will trick his victim into ingesting. Once the concoction is taken, the victim would begin to cough up blood, be horribly ill with a fever and seemingly die, having no signs of life. After this horrific show, the Bokor waits for the person to be declared legally dead and buried according to custom. After the funeral, this dark practitioner would return to the gravesite under cover of night, dig up the body and wait for the victim to "awaken" from their drugged coma. Unfortunately, upon waking, the victims were no longer free men; instead they were beaten into submission and taken away as slaves to the home of the Bokor, or to a buyer of slaves. From this point on, the victims are given a daily dose of another concoction that keeps them in a drugged stupor; able to function as workers, but having no memory of anything else and no desire to flee, as they know nothing beyond their basic needs and the orders of their new master.

The most famous documented case of someone surviving enslavement as a "zombie", is the story of Clairvius Narcisse. In the 1960's, Narcisse claims that he was poisoned and zombified by a Bokor that his own brother had hired to get him out of the way for personal reasons. In the reports, Narcisse had gone to a hospital claiming that he felt very ill with a fever and other symptoms. He was dismissed with a minor diagnosis but was later found and declared dead by two physicians. As the story goes, Narcisse recalled that after he "died" he could hear everything going on around his lifeless body; the doctor's voice, his family crying, even the sounds of being buried. He soon woke up to a voodoo priest pulling him out of the ground and beating him into full consciousness. Narcisse was taken away to be enslaved on a farm, where he was kept drugged and zombified for nearly 20 years of his life. After 20 years had passed, the Bokor died and Narcisse was finally freed from the drug dosages and able to leave the farm, seeking his family.

Zombies have appeared in many novels and film adaptations over the years. There are a small number of films that follow the Bokor version, such as the 1932 movie, *White Zombie*, starring Bela Lugosi. Most zombie films, however, follow the science fiction version, which is quite different, with their reanimated, rotting corpses having no conscious thought, other than their intense hunger for human flesh. Rather than being drugged and enslaved as zombies, these monsters are usually created through a pandemic infection or a science experiment gone wrong. *These* hideous creatures are not ruled by a Bokor, rather, they are enslaved to their own carnivorous appetite, as they can think of nothing else.

The earliest influential examples in zombie fiction are films such as *White Zombie*, *Night of the living dead*, and *Herbert West–Reanimator*. From these creatures, more and more stories and films have emerged, evolving the zombie into the creature of classic horror that we know them as today… rotting, grotesque, walking dead, forever in search of braaains!

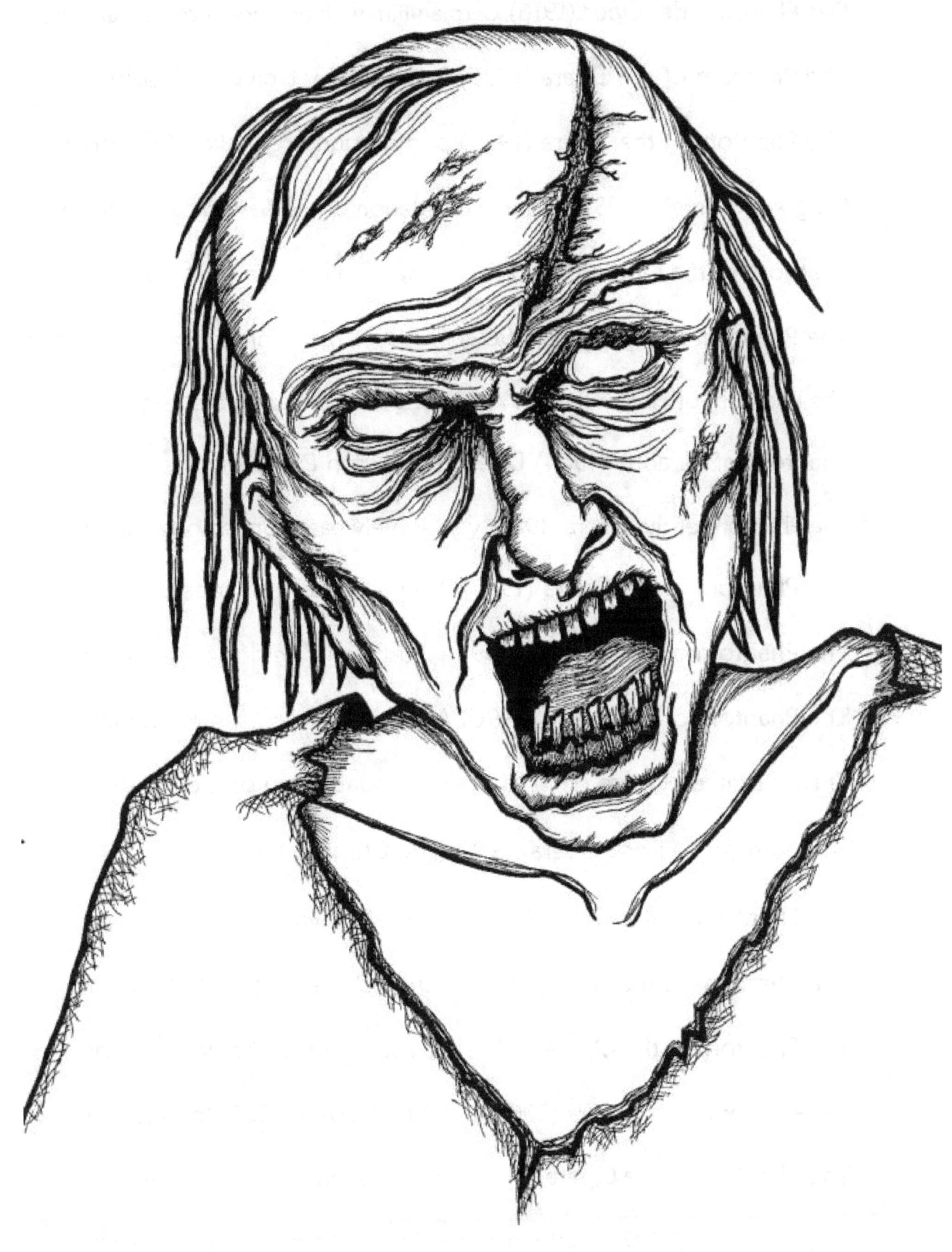

41

Das Phantom der Oper (1916) German film with no known copies surviving

The Phantom of the Opera (1925) Produced by Universal Studios

The Phantom of the Opera (1929) partial sound re-make of the original

Song At Midnight (1937) Chinese adaptation of the Gaston Leroux novel

Phantom of the Opera (1943) loosely based on the Gaston Leroux novel

The Phantom of the Opera (1962) produced by Hammer Film Productions

The Phantom of Hollywood (1974) very loosely based on the original novel

Phantom of Paradise (1974) Directed by Brian De Palma

The Phantom of the Opera (1983) very loosely based on the original novel

The Phantom of the Opera (1987) Animated cartoon adaptation

The Phantom of the Opera (1989) a much gorier version of the classic tale

The Phantom of the Opera (1990) A two-part television miniseries

O Fantasma da Ópera (1991) a Brazilian adaptation of the story

Phantom of the Rock Opera (1991) The Chipmunks S7/E10

The Phantom of the Opera (1998) Originally Il Fantasma dell'Opera

The Phantom of the Megaplex (2000) A Disney channel original movie

The Phantom of the Opera (2004) an adaptation of the 1986 musical

The Phantom of the Opera (2004) HBO first look S11/E25 Documentary

The Phantom of the Opera (2005) A musical adaptation of the novel

Angel of Music (2009) an aftermath tale loosely based on the original story

Phantom of the Opera

The Phantom of the opera is a tale of both love and horror. It is the story of a young couple falling in love, with the jealousy of a deformed madman working to keep them apart. The beginning of this story is a seduction of beautiful music, though it ends in violence and sorrow.

As a child, Christine's father tells her many stories of the Phantom of the Opera, although he calls him, instead, the *Angel of Music*. As her father tells her of the "angel's" heavenly voice and skill with instruments, Christine is enchanted, with a growing admiration and curiosity that follows her into adulthood. As a young woman, she is given a position in the chorus at the Paris opera house, Palais Garnier, where she has so often imagined this *Angel of Music*. Christine begins to hear the most beautiful voice echoing through the halls very soon after she arrives and immediately thinks of her father's stories. She asks the voice if he is in fact the Angel of Music, the one she has heard so many stories of. The voice affirms that he is this angel and he offers to teach her all that he knows.

With these lessons, Christine's music grows to be quite heavenly, in its own right. She takes what she has learned and performs at the big gala, enthralling the audience with her beauty and talent. One member of the audience is Christine's childhood playmate, Raoul, who remembers her voice and his deep love for her is rekindled. Before the boy can claim her for his own, Christine is spirited away to the Phantom's home, beneath the opera house. He reveals that his true name as Erik and that he plans to keep her there for himself; secretly hoping that she will fall in love with him. Christine does, in fact, start to feel affection towards this musical genius, with all his romantic passion and talent. Erik is hopeful that she has finally come to love him, but when Christine removes his mask, she is instantly repulsed by the grotesquely deformed features hidden beneath and she begs for him to release her.

Erik fears that he has lost Christine's favor for good and, in a moment of madness, he decides that he will keep her prisoner permanently; if he can't have her, neither can Raoul. After a couple of weeks, with Christine pleading for her freedom, he finally agrees to release her, but only if she will wear his ring and promise to be faithful to him. Christine agrees.

After her release, Christine secretly meets with Raoul on the rooftop, telling him of all that has happened to her beneath the opera house, with Erik. Raoul promises that he will take her far away, where Erik will never find her or harm her again. Christine happily agrees to run away with him, while Erik is secretly listening and making his very different plans.

Erik's obsession had begun with him secretly terrorizing anyone who came between himself and Christine, or anyone that interfered with her career. But, with this betrayal, he becomes bolder in his violence, imprisoning Raoul and taking Christine to the cellars once again. He threatens to blow up the entire theater, killing them all, if she will not agree to marry him. Against her heart's desire, Christine does agree to marry Erik, wishing to save everyone involved. In a jealous rage, Erik still tries to drown Raoul, so that he can never come between them again, but Christine begs him to spare the boy, as she promises to be only his, forever. In the end, he spares Raoul and releases Christine, telling her to go marry the man that she truly loves. He makes her promise only one thing; that when he dies she must return to bury him.

The Phantom of the Opera is a classic horror novel, created by the French writer, Gaston Leroux, in 1909. The novel was not overly popular and did not sell very well; it was even taken out of print several times in its earlier years. It did much better on stage and in film than it ever did as a work of literature. The most notable screen adaptation for *Phantom of the Opera* was the 1925 silent black and white film, produced by Universal Studios, starring Lon Chaney as Erik and Mary Philbin as Christine. Another memorable performance was on stage in Andrew Lloyd Webber's 1986 musical *Phantom of the Opera*. This adaptation first opened in London's West End in 1986 and was also performed in 1988 on Broadway, among many other showings. Both adaptations were well-received and gained positive reviews, taking a previously uncelebrated book and transforming it into a story that has become quite significant in the genre of classic horror and theater performances.

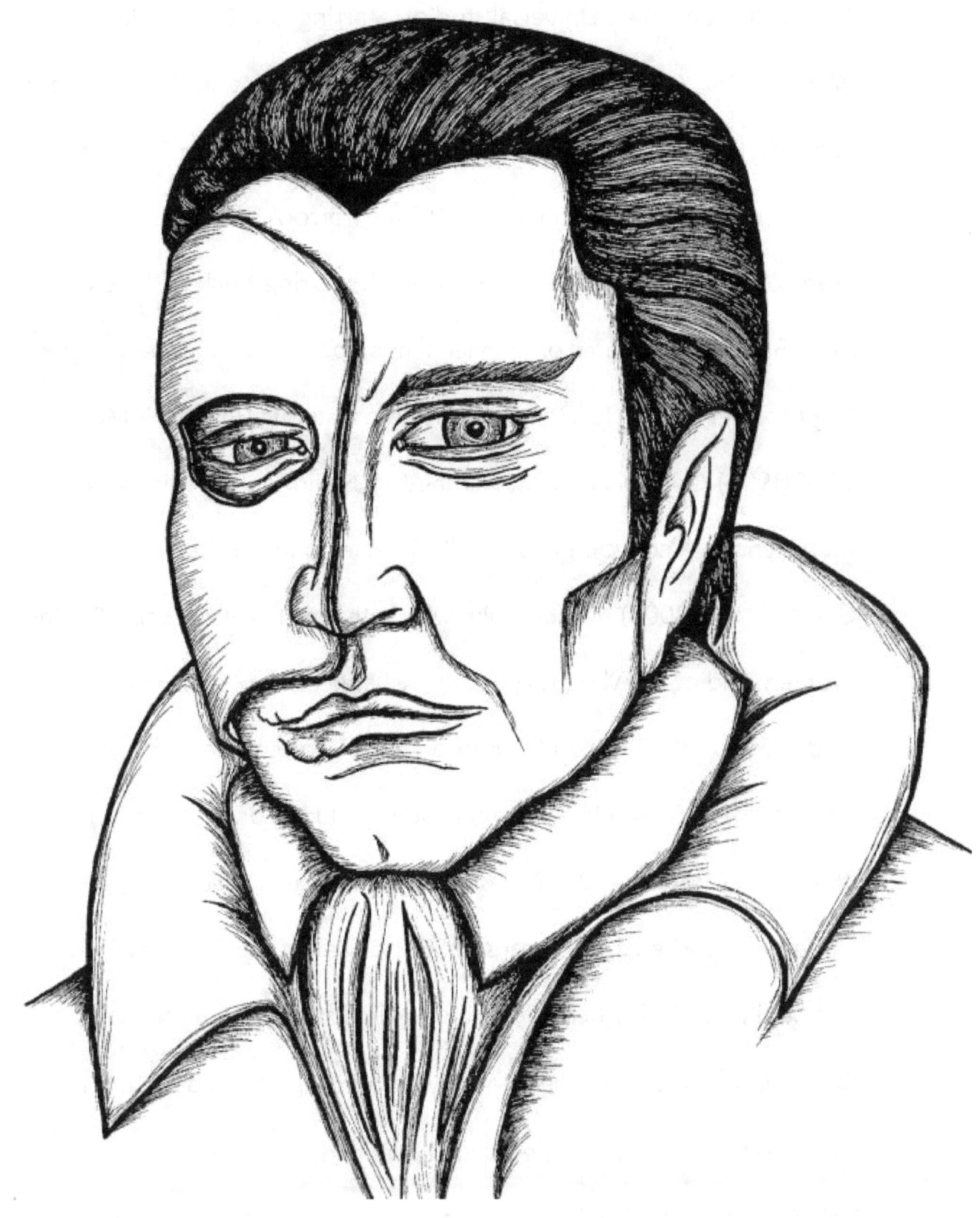

Werewolf of London (1935) Universal studios, Starring Henry Hull

The Wolf Man (1941) Universal studios, Starring Lon Chaney Jr

Wolfen (1981) Orion Pictures, Starring Albert Finney and Diane Venora

The Howling (1981) Based on the novel by Gary Brandner

An American Werewolf in London (1981) horror/comedy

Teen Wolf (1985) Directed by Rod Daniel, Starring Michael J. Fox

Silver Bullet (1985) based on Stephen King's novella Cycle of the Werewolf

The Monster Squad (1987) Tri-Star Pictures, featuring Universal's Monsters

Wolf (1994) Columbia Pictures, Starring Jack Nicholson and Michelle Pfeiffer

An American Werewolf in Paris (1997) sequel to the 1981 London version

Ginger Snaps (2000) Canadian film with Katharine Isabelle & Emily Perkins

Brotherhood of the Wolf (2001) loosely based on the 18th century killings

Underworld (2003) a film focused on both Vampires and Lycans

Van Helsing (2004) a tribute to the Universal Horror Monster films

Blood and Chocolate (2007) based on Annette Curtis Klause's novel

Underworld: Rise of the Lycans (2009) origins of the Vampire–Lycan war

The Wolfman (2010) Remake of the 1941 classic by the same name

Red Riding Hood (2011) very loosely based on Little Red Riding Hood

Werewolf: The Beast Among Us (2012) filmed in Romania

The Twilight Saga (2008-2012) based on the Stephenie Meyer novels

Werewolves

The Werewolf, also known as the Lycanthrope (Greek for wolf man), is described as a human being who shape-shifts into a wolf, as the result of a curse or magic. Not just any wolf though, with the werewolf being much larger and much more powerful, with a speed that far surpasses any human or natural animal. In some cultures, it is believed that you can tell a werewolf from an ordinary wolf by these attributes and also by its tail, or the lack thereof; having no tail was believed to be a characteristic of a witch or demon in animal form.

There are many legends on how the werewolf curse originally began. Some legends say that if you drink rainwater out of the footprint of an animal on the full moon then you will be cursed into the form of that beast. The oldest tale of the werewolf, however, says that the curse came directly from the gods themselves as a punishment. In Greek mythology, there is the story of Lycaon, king of Arcadia, who wanted to test his guest, Zeus, to see if he truly was a god. To test for the all-knowing power of the divine, Lycaon slaughters one of his own sons and serves the human flesh to Zeus, as they dine together that evening. He believes that Zeus will reveal himself as only mortal by unknowingly eating the taboo flesh. Of course, Zeus is outraged at Lycaon's attempt to trick him and so he punishes the whole family by turning King Lycaon and his fifty sons into wolves, thus creating the original werewolf family and founding fathers of the curse. And so, the werewolf curse was then passed down generation to generation through bloodlines or through infection, by biting or scratching. *There are many other versions of this story*

The fear and persecution of werewolves was not only one of legend, but a very real occurrence. Beginning in the early 15th century and subsiding in the 18th century, there was a werewolf hysteria that spread, much the old witch hunts. There were numerous trials, where people were accused of being werewolves and thus sentenced to die for their unnatural and unholy state of being. One example occurred in 1598, when two children were attacked and killed while in the forest picking berries. Villagers who came upon the scene, saw young Pernette Gandillon, dirty and blood-splattered, running away on all fours like an animal. The wild girl was caught and imprisoned, while her brother and their other sister were taken in and questioned. Allegedly, the siblings confessed to being in league with a witch who gave them magical salves to put on their bodies, so they would become wolves. Subsequently, the whole family was found guilty and sentenced to death by burning. However, this and other cases were later assumed to simply have been signs of madness. This mental illness was later labeled as Clinical Lycanthropy; a rare psychiatric syndrome where the afflicted person believes they can transform into an animal, be it wolf or other such things.

During this time, when the curse was believed to truly exist, there were also quests for ways to cure the affliction. In the middle ages, they believed that the *original* werewolves could not be cured, but that those who had been infected could be saved. Wolf's bane was thought to be one remedy for the ailment, while others believed that an exorcism was necessary, as if to expel the evil beast within. Another cure was through a brutal surgical procedure, where the afflicted person rarely survived.

When the attempted cures failed, or was not an option, the only other solution was to destroy the accursed beast. In literature, it is often said that the werewolf is vulnerable to silver, and that you can kill one with a silver bullet. However, in classical lycanthrope stories, werewolves are not affected by weapons of any kind, whether they are silver or not. In the oldest of stories, it is said that the only way to kill a werewolf is by severing the head from its body, removing his heart and burning the remains of the beast into ash.

*Other werewolf cases in history that you might research online are those of Peter Stumpp, The tailor of Chalons, Jacques Roulet the Werewolf of Angers, Jean Grenier at Bordeaux, The Beast of Gévaudan and Gilles Garnier in Dole.

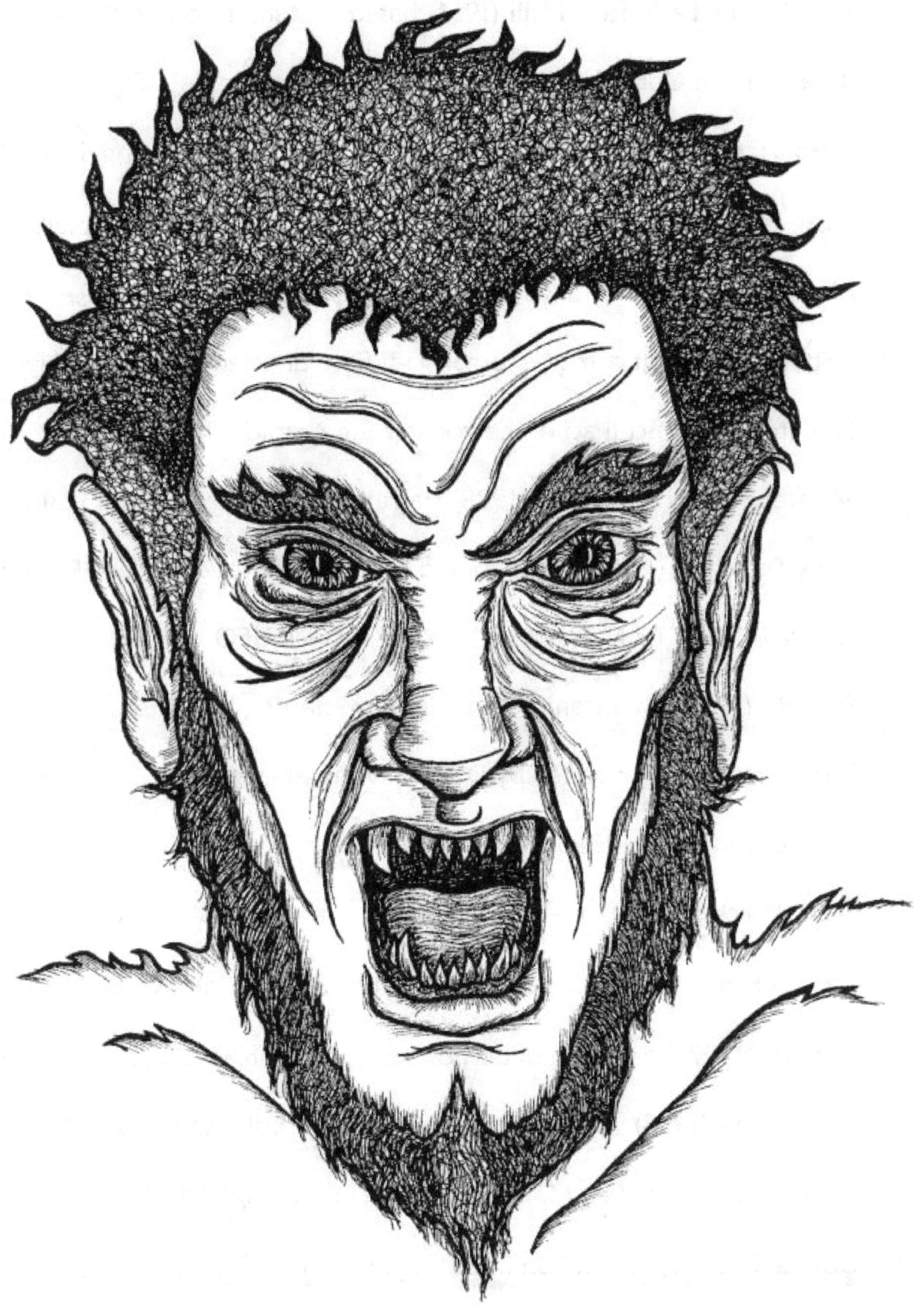

The Day the Earth Stood Still (1951) based on a short story by Harry Bates

It Came from Outer Space (1953) Universal's first film in 3-D

Earth vs. the Flying Saucers (1956) Aka Invasion of the Flying Saucers

Close Encounters of the Third Kind (1977) Directed by Steven Spielberg

Alien (1979) Featuring alien designs by Swiss surrealist artist H. R. Giger

Critters (1986) cult comedy horror sci-fi film, directed by Stephen Herek

Predator (1987) Sci-fi action horror starring Arnold Schwarzenegger

My Stepmother Is an Alien (1988) starring Dan Aykroyd & Kim Basinger

Body Snatchers (1993) loosely based on the 1955 novel by Jack Finney

Roswell (1994) TV Movie based on the Roswell UFO incident in 1947

Stargate (1994) American-French sci-fi film, starring Kurt Russell

The Arrival (1996) directed by David Twohy, starring Charlie Sheen

Independence Day (1996) A military sci-fi movie with an all-star cast

Mars Attacks! (1996) directed by Tim Burton with an all-star cast

Men in Black (1997) based on The Men in Black comic book series

Contact (1997) adaptation of the novel by Carl Sagan, starring Jodie Foster

The Faculty (1998) written by Kevin Williamson, starring Elijah Wood

Signs (2002) written by M. Night Shyamalan, starring Mel Gibson

District 9 (2009) adaptation from the short film Alive in Joburg

Aliens

By definition, *Alien* is the name that we have given to people, creatures or things that are foreign and unfamiliar to us. Universally speaking, this means creatures that are not native to our planet, Earth; also known as extraterrestrials. These otherworldly beings, or the idea of them, has been a great source of curiosity throughout history. They have been portrayed widely, all over the world, in movies, books, as well as primitive and modern art. While the true image of the extraterrestrial is somewhat of a mystery, the film and literature industry has offered its own interpretations, illustrating aliens in many ways. These fictional images range from scary reptilian looking creatures, to the most popular version, with its large eyes, large head and a slender body. We have even illustrated them to look like ourselves; as a human-like being, trying to blend in with our species. While these images vary widely, a few aspects do remain the same; aliens are almost always portrayed as having higher intelligence, greater capabilities, and an intense interest in humans and our planet—though their interests vary from peaceful to violent conquest.

While these descriptions and film portrayals feel very real, there is no hard, scientific evidence to prove or disprove the existence of alien lifeforms beyond earth. However, the number of witness accounts and stories are endless, all over the world. Throughout history there have been numerous alleged UFO sightings and claims of alien abduction; most of which are simply dismissed as hoaxes, hallucinations, or sightings of other earth-based and explainable flying objects.

In 1947 the most well-known, documented UFO incident took place when a foreign, airborne object crashed on a ranch near Roswell, New Mexico. According to the local newspapers, the rancher went to the authorities, claiming that a flying saucer had crashed on his property. The man later claimed that the army came and recovered the flying disc, taking it to their headquarters where it was never seen again. Soon after,

51

the military made a public statement, claiming that there was no "flying saucer" and that it had only been a misguided weather balloon. Some people accepted this statement as fact, while others believed that the government was covering up the truth. Honestly, the Roswell conspiracy theory is much more than one could ever do it justice in such a brief writing, but there are many newspaper articles and witness accounts available online for further research in this and other UFO experiences.

It is unproven, but possible, that alien sightings go back even further than the Roswell incident; possibly even extending into ancient historical accounts, through some of the oldest known cave drawings. During these ancient times, according to research, cave paintings were not done simply for aesthetic enjoyment. Rather, they were believed to be based on real-life occurrences; the primitive interpretations of things that the artist saw and experienced around them. In Guatemala, for example, some people believe that the sculptures and images of the flying turtles were possibly the artist's way of explaining the sighting of a flying disc-shaped object. Another example is the Aboriginal cave paintings in Australia of the Wondjina; cloud and rain spirits, who in their primitive art form are said to resemble aliens or astronauts in space helmets. Throughout the world there are many other ancient depictions of possible UFO's, as well as written works that have been interpreted in favor of alien existence; biblical scriptures, like the book of Ezekiel, for example.

As you can see, without any hard evidence, there are still many people who choose to believe in the real existence of aliens, even today, finding their own "proof" in stories and historical clues. But, no matter which way you choose to view them, as fact or fiction, they can be quite an intimidating possibility. With their strange appearance, superior intelligence and mysterious motives, it's no wonder that they are in the spotlight of many horror films. Perhaps they simply appear saying, "I come in peace", OR maybe, as portrayed in popular horror fiction, they are vicious planetary warlords, looking to take over the universe by force and mass destruction. With so much mystery surrounding them, the possibilities are boundless, making these creatures perfect for science fiction and a definite mark in classic horror history!

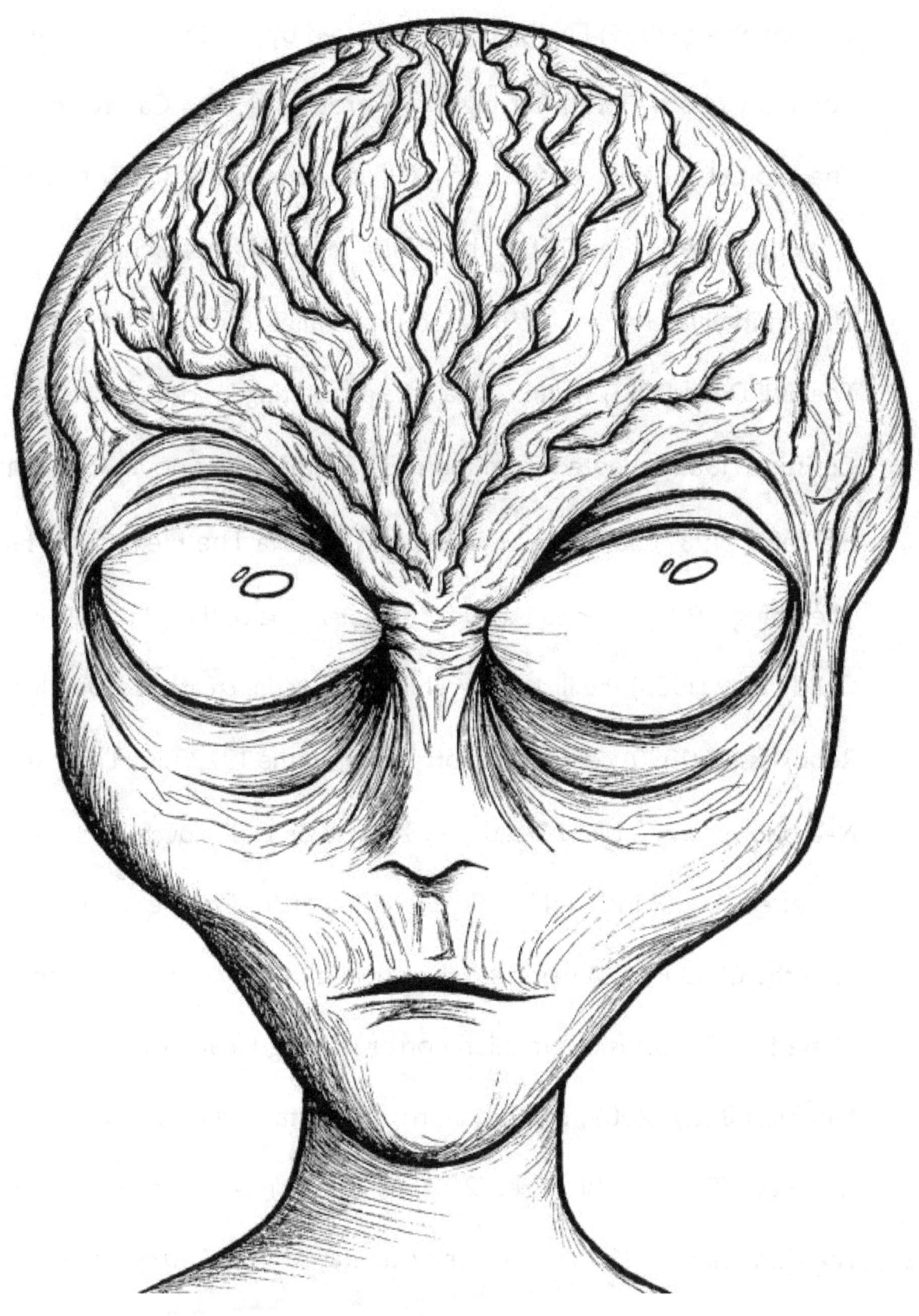

Häxan (1922) film by Danish filmmaker Benjamin Christensen

The She-Beast (1965) English bride possessed by an 18th-century witch

Rosemary's Baby (1968) starring Mia Farrow and John Cassavetes

The Exorcist (1973) adapted from William Peter Blatty's 1971 novel

The Omen (1976) The first of three films in The Omen series

The Amityville Horror (1979) based on an alleged real-life experience

The Evil Dead (1981) written by Sam Raimi, starring Bruce Campbell

Christine (1983) adapted from the 1983 Stephen King novel Christine

Hellraiser (1987) based on Clive Barker's novella The Hellbound Heart

The Thing (1982) Directed by John Carpenter, one of three in a trilogy

Child's Play (1988) the first in the Child's Play series created by Don Mancini

Repossessed (1990) comedy spoofs based on the 1973 film The Exorcist

Necronomicon: Book of Dead (1993) based on H. P. Lovecraft stories

Possessed (2000) inspired by the exorcism case of Robbie Mannheim

Bless the Child (2000) based on the novel by Cathy Cash Spellman

Blessed (2004) British-Romanian horror starring Heather Graham

Jennifer's Body (2009) comedy-horror film, starring Megan Fox

Anneliese: The Exorcist Tapes (2011) based on Anneliese Michel's exorcism

The Conjuring (2013) based on the true story of the Perron family

Demons

Demons are widely defined as malevolent spirits, evil deities or even as fallen angels. They are described in many ways, but in art and literature they are most often illustrated with horns atop their head, hairy animal-like bodies and cloven hooves for feet, like that of a satyr. In the bible, however, the demon called Satan is depicted quite differently. In *Revelations*, he is described more than once as a "...dragon, that ancient serpent, who is the devil". In the Garden of Eden, he is depicted once more as a serpent, lurking in the apple tree as he tempts Eve with the fruit of knowledge. In earlier scriptures, however, he is contrastingly described as being the most beautiful of angels in heaven—before having fallen from grace. In the book of Ezekiel, he was said to be "...the seal of perfection, full of wisdom and perfect in beauty", the greatest of god's angels until "wickedness" was found in him and he was cast forth.

The origins of the demon spirit vary by culture and religious belief, although there are similarities throughout each. Before Christianity, the Greeks believed in their many gods, one of which was Hades, who ruled the dark depths of the earth, just as with Satan. However, unlike Satan, Hades was not portrayed to be evil and was not forced from his fellow gods as a punishment; he had simply drawn lots with his siblings, and so, was given rule of the underworld. There are stories more like that of Satan's in the Islamic belief, with spirits called Jinn; both good Jinn and evil Jinn (devils). Iblis was one of the first Jinn and is much like the Christian version of Satan. Iblis disobeyed Allah, refusing to acknowledge a lesser creature that was made of "clay" (humans). For this, Iblis was cast out and condemned to dwell in hell, where he vowed to bring all of Allah's precious mankind down with him.

The rebellion of evil against good has been a recurring theme with deities throughout history and cultures worldwide. However, this battle of wills was not limited to wreaking havoc only in the spirit realm. Many believe that evil lurks in and among humans every day, in accordance to the stories that often portray demons as being jealous over the creation of humans. With this belief of evil walking among people, comes the idea of demonic possession; the control of an individual by a malevolent spirit. Characteristics of a supposed demonic possession are memory loss, convulsions, fainting, speaking in foreign languages unknown to the victim, changes in tone of voice, mysterious scratches or bite marks and inhuman strength. The victim is said to have no control over their body or mind until the demon is expelled, by way of exorcism. The oldest known references to demonic possession and exorcism comes from the Sumerians. In this culture, it was believed that all diseases were caused by demons called Gidim, also known as a shade. The priests would attempt to expel the Gidim by performing a ritual exorcism, using certain prayers that have been found inscribed on ancient cuneiform tablets.

There are many documented cases of demonic possession, some of which have come to be the basis for many horror films. In 1976 Anneliese Michel, a German Catholic woman, was claimed to be possessed and underwent an exorcism to be rid of the supposed demon. At sixteen years of age, Anneliese had been diagnosed and was suffering from recurring epileptic seizures. After her diagnosis, she became increasingly depressed and was eventually admitted to a psychiatric hospital for treatment. Anneliese got much worse; at some point, she even became intolerant of certain religious objects and claimed that she was hearing voices. Medications were not helping her condition and, as the ailment only got worse with particular symptoms, her family was soon convinced that she was possessed. They quickly appealed for an exorcism which they received after much hesitation from the church. Anneliese died soon after the rites were performed. Investigations revealed that the young woman had been severely malnourished and dehydrated; her parents and the priests claimed that she refused to eat and vomited, but were still charged with negligence and sentenced accordingly. This case attracted much public attention and was eventually the basis for the 2005 movie, *The Exorcism of Emily Rose,* starring Jennifer Carpenter and Tom Wilkinson.

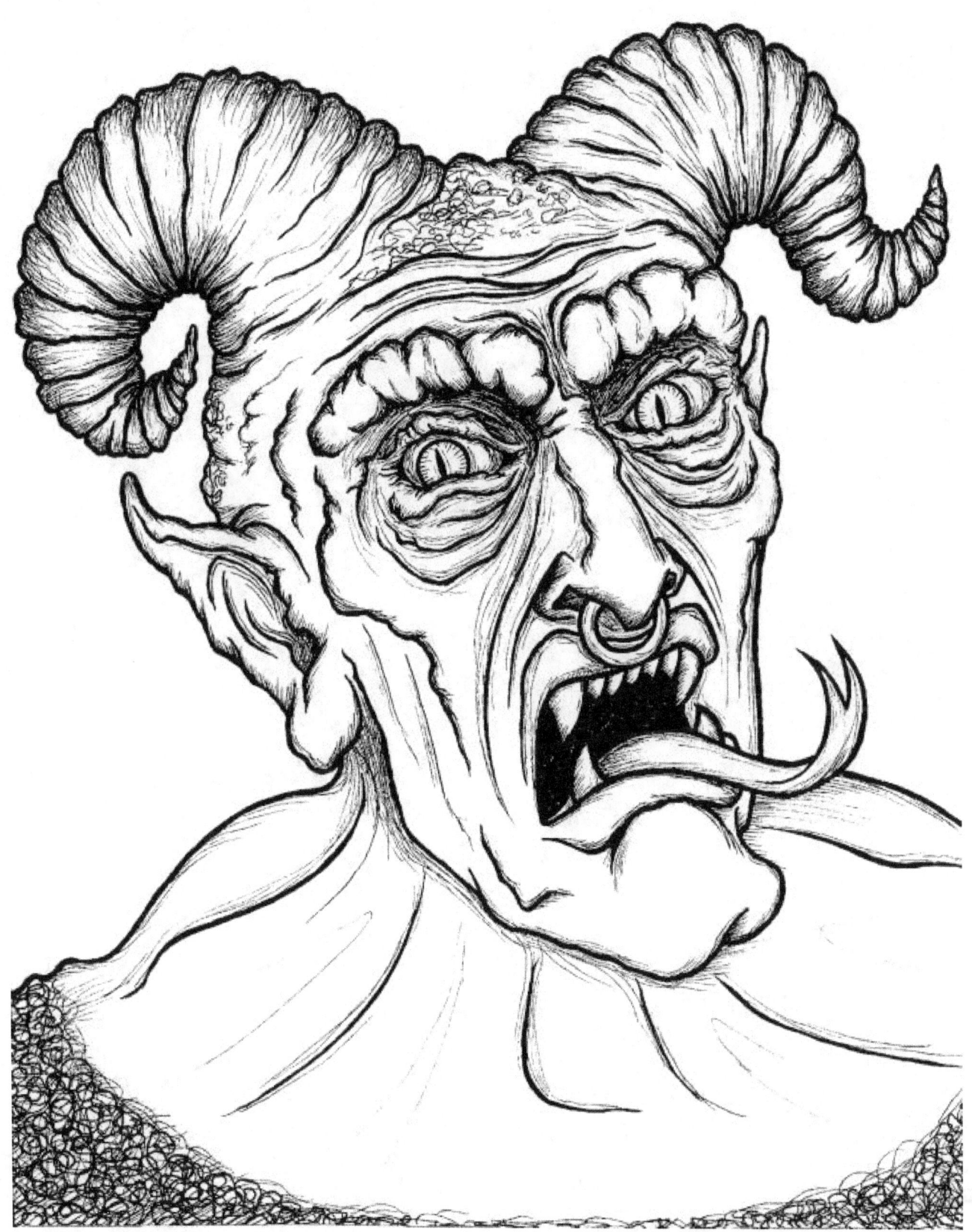

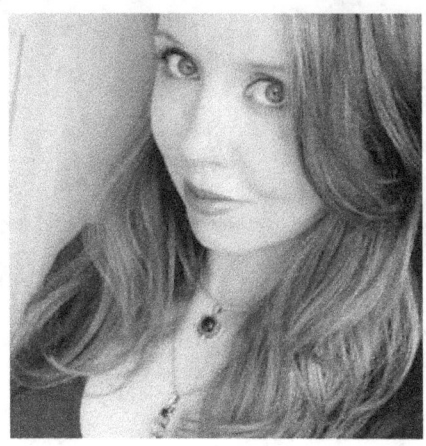

Davina Rush is an entrepreneur, an author and an artist. She writes Gothic Supernatural fiction, as well as Educational Coloring Books which she illustrates by hand. She runs a small business as a Personal Organizer, manages a local Supernatural Writer's Group called, Monsters and Maidens, and she works hard every day to raise her two beautiful daughters.

Born in Northwest Florida, 1978, Davina has also lived in Massachusetts and Tennessee, before returning to settle once more in Florida, near her family. During her time in Tennessee, Davina attended Chattanooga State College, where she studied art and literature. These two subjects have been a constant passion throughout all her life; from elementary school to college and later continuing her practice and studies independently. Her greatest literary influences have been Lewis Carroll, C.S. Lewis, J.R.R. Tolkien, Neil Gaiman, Stephen King, J.K. Rowling, Susan Hill and Marion Zimmer Bradley.

Davina enjoys oil painting and assemblage art, though her main career focus is in writing and ink-illustration. Her current publications include four educational coloring books, a handful of Gothic short stories and on inspirational book. The complete collection of her titles can be found on Amazon.com or at DavinaRush.com. For more information or to contact the author, please join her on Facebook, Twitter, Instagram or Patreon.

Note from the Author

I hope you have enjoyed your coloring and learning experience with the *Creatures of Classic Horror*, as much as I enjoyed creating this publication for you!

In October of 2012 I celebrated Halloween as I always do; decorating the house in spooky splendor, getting dressed up, taking my kids out trick-or-treating and watching all our favorite, kid-friendly Halloween movies. After the little ones went off to bed, I continued Halloween with my own, grownup movie marathon. I watched all my usual Halloween favorites; Frankenstein, Sleepy Hollow, Bram Stoker's Dracula and a few others. Inspired by my favorite movie monsters, I started to draw a pencil sketch of Frankenstein and his bride just for fun (a sketch that still hangs on my wall). As always, once I begin one art project, the creative wheels start turning and something else pops up— ah, the muse and her whispers! On that very night, with Frankenstein on the television and flowing from my pencil, I knew what my next coloring book would be! My favorite monsters, the classics forefathers of horror, would be gathered together with all the fun information I could find on them; the history and folklore, fun facts and even a movie list for your further entertainment.

I think that this book has easily been my favorite writing/art/research project to date. I truly have had so much fun creating this collection! I hope you will enjoy my efforts here and I would love to know what you think. Please feel free to email me anytime with your comments through Facebook.com/DavinaRush. You can also leave reviews on the website in which you purchased this book. All feedback is welcome and greatly appreciated. For more information about myself, as well as updates on my latest publications, events, contests and more, please visit my website at www.DavinaRush.com